Hardcover - 979-8-9867482-5-2
Paperback - 979-8-9867482-3-8
eBook - 979-8-9867482-4-5

This book belongs to

THIS BOOK IS DEDICATED TO MY CHILDREN – MY CURIOUS GENIUSES

THANK YOU BOYS FOR GIVING ME THE OPPORTUNITY TO LEARN AND GROW WITH YOU!

MY SPOUSE WHO SUPPORTS ME IN ALL MY ENDEAVORS

WE ARE THE BOOKS WE READ
AND THE THINGS WE LOVE.

– CATH CROWLEY

Rafa loved his family's food.
It put him in the best mood!

But the kids at school made a face
Whenever Rafa had a taste.

"I won't try that.
No, no way!
It Smells so strange!"
Jake would say.

Rafa felt very sad.
He knew his food did not
taste bad!

Mediterranean Sea
Egypt
Arabia
Somalia

But when at home,
The smell of food helped his
imagination roam!

Rafa imagined how his food and culture traveled to new shores in the ancient days

He even imagined being an
explorer on the sea,
Rafa felt like royalty!

The next day, Rafa asked his teacher if the class could have a World Food Day!

His teacher agreed!
"What an awesome idea,
indeed!"

Rafa was super excited about World Food Day.

At home, he helped his mommy cook.
My mommy didn't even need a recipe book!
She sprinkled her magic,
Making my favorite chicken curry.

We made some rice, and samosas, too.
Mom always knew just what to do.

But behind the excitement, Rafa was a bit scared.

"What if my friends wouldn't care about the food I'd share?"

Recipe

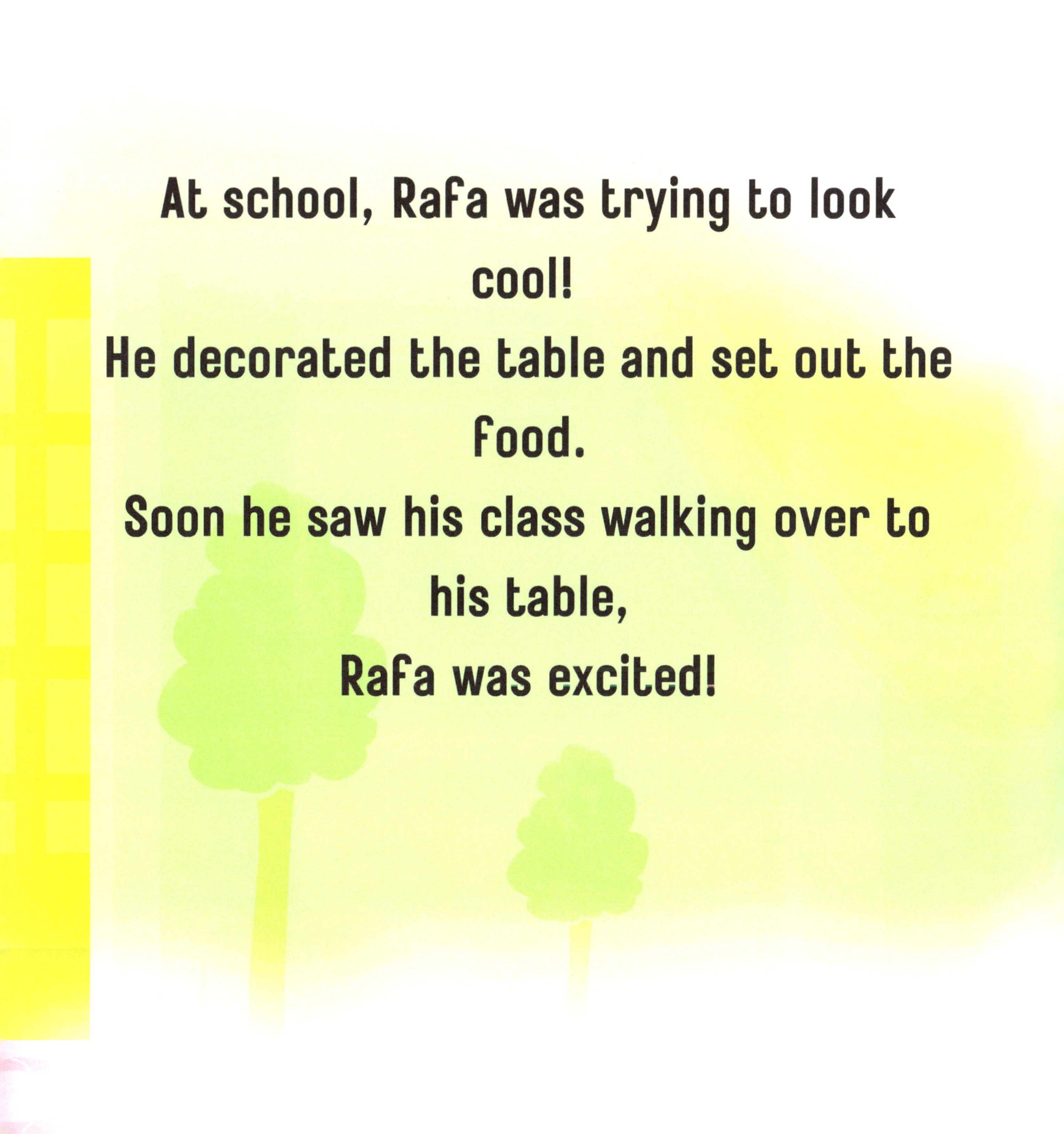

At school, Rafa was trying to look cool!

He decorated the table and set out the food.

Soon he saw his class walking over to his table,

Rafa was excited!

The class followed the yummy smell.
As Rafa saw them come, He proudly
presented his food,
and he had a story to tell.

All ears listened as Rafa spoke.

He told the history of his culture
and food,
and how amazing the flavors
made him feel.

Everybody tasted the food Rafa brought in.

He felt great when he saw their grin!

Just then Jake walked over to Rafa and said "I'm sorry, Rafa,"

"The food is amazing! And It's my new favorite thing to eat.

Thanks for sharing your culture and this great treat."

Rafa was very happy that day.

Then, as all the aroma hung in the air,
Rafa was proud that he could share.

And he whispered to himself

I love curry
and I'm not sorry!

The END

Curry was a blanket term for Indian food invented by the British during the time when the British ruled India (1858 - 1947).

It is the anglicized version of the Tamil word Kari, meaning sauce

Calling all Indian food - "Curry" can be a culturally insensitive thing to say!

Coriander Powder
Garam Masala
Red Chilli Powder
Mustard Seeds
Turmeric Powder
Saffron
Bay Leaves
Cumin Powder
Fenugreek
Black Pepper
Poppy Seeds
Cardamom
Cinnamon
Dry Ginger
Star Anise
Cloves
Saunf

Cultural Facts

Indian foods have a recipe - specific spice blends.
Indian cuisine is made up of a variety of dishes from
sauces or curry-based to
Lentil soup called Dal,
Saag - which can have a Vegetable base
Sambar, Samosa - a vegetable dumpling,
Naan and many rice dishes with spice blends such as
Biryani, Curd rice, Sambar Rice.. and more.

Indian Food is not equal to Curry,
Curry is not equal to Indian food

It is a small part of the vast variety of dishes in the
Indian Cuisine

"Through my books, I intend to help our future leaders build on their social-cultural skills which are key to becoming inclusive members of our community and great (future) leaders!"

ERLIN KAKKANAD - Author

Thank you for making my book part of your family.

I am passionate about bringing awareness to cultural and ethnic diversity through stories from my lived experience in India and USA.

Other titles that you will like

Happy in your Skin

Is Rafa Different

Written by

Erlin Kakkanad

Please send in feedback here:

erlinkakkanad@gmail.com

Written by
Erlin Kakkanad

Illustrated by
Muskan Baldodia

HAPPY IN YOUR SKIN

Is Rafa Different?

Rafa Loves coloring

let's color!

Be Kind and
Color
along!

www.ingramcontent.com/pod-product-compliance
Ingram Content Group UK Ltd.
Pitfield, Milton Keynes, MK11 3LW, UK
UKHW061031310726
14089UKWH00009B/194
* 9 7 9 8 9 8 6 7 4 8 2 5 2 *